# M is for Mitten

## A Michigan Alphabet

Written by Annie Appleford, Poems by Kathy-jo Wargin and Illustrated by Michael G. Monroe

Sleeping Bear Press™
310 North Main Street, Suite 300
Chelsea, MI 48118
www.sleepingbearpress.com

© 2005 Sleeping Bear Press is an imprint of Gale, a part of Cengage Learning.

Printed and bound in China.

20  19  18  17  16  15  14  13

Appleford, Annie.

M is for mitten : a Michigan alphabet book / by Annie Appleford; illustrated by Michael Monroe.
p. cm.
Summary: Presents for each letter of the alphabet something associated with the state of Michigan, from "apple blossom" to "Detroit Zoo."

ISBN 978-1-886947-73-3
1. Michigan Juvenile literature.  2. English language—Alphabet Juvenile literature. [1. Michigan.  2. Alphabet.] I. Monroe, F566.3.A66 1999
[E]—dc21
99-33497
CIP

For Mike, Maggie, and Ben with my love.
Thanks to my family, friends,
Pearly Broome, Michael Monroe, Kathy-jo Wargin,
and Sleeping Bear Press.
A. A.


Thanks to my parents for giving me the
confidence in myself to pursue my dream
of being an artist, and to my grandparents
for inspiring me with my first paint set.
M. G. M.

The apple blossom is the state flower of Michigan. In late spring, this delicate flower blossoms with five pink and white petals.

A is for the Apple blossom,
frilly as can be.
It dances in the springtime breeze
upon the apple tree.

a

A

The Mackinac Bridge connects the Upper and Lower Peninsulas of Michigan. It spans five miles over an area of water known as the Straits of Mackinac, which is where Lake Michigan and Lake Huron meet. One of the longest suspension bridges in the world, taking over three years to build, "the Mighty Mac" opened to traffic in 1957. Before that, people traveled back and forth by boat.

The brook trout is a small, colorful fish. It likes to swim in shallow lakes and streams. It is the state fish of Michigan and has red, green, and blue spots on its sides.

B is for a great big Bridge
that's called "the Mighty Mac."
Whichever side you may be on
you can drive across and back.

Cherry trees grow in long, neat rows in the light, sandy soil of northern Michigan. There are so many orchards near Traverse City that it has become known as "the Cherry Capital of the World." Western Lower Michigan is ideal for growing fruit such as cherries, apples, and peaches because Lake Michigan warms the passing air in spring and fall, and cools it in the summer, causing more moderate temperatures.

Now C is for Cherry.
Little sweet ones fill my belly.
Tart ones make me pucker,
so they're used in jam and jelly.

Do you see anything else on this page that begins with the letter C?

Detroit is the largest city in our state. It was founded in 1701 by Antoine de la Mothe Cadillac, and was first called Fort Pontchartrain du Detroit. Known as "the Automobile Capital of the World," Detroit is home to General Motors, Ford, and Daimler-Chrysler. It was the first city in the world to pave a mile of concrete road and to install a traffic light. But Detroit is famous for more than just cars. It was also the birthplace of a record company called "Motown," where many famous singers got their start.

Did you know Detroit (de troit) is the French word for strait, meaning a narrow passage of water connecting two larger bodies of water?

D is for Detroit.
It's called the Motor City,
where cars roll out of factories,
so bright and new and pretty.

Eastern white pine starts with E,
a tree so tall and straight,
cut for timber long ago
all throughout our state.

We've had fun from A to E.
What is next?
Look and see!

The eastern white pine, Michigan's state tree, is very tall and straight, making it a good choice for timber. Michigan was filled with white pine when the first European settlers came, and soon these and other newcomers began to harvest the trees in an era of the 1800s called "The Big Cut." In the 1870s enough eastern white pine was cut that if placed end to end it would have made a path from Michigan to the moon.

Ee

F stands for Gerald R. Ford.
He was president long ago.
He is a very special man
from Michigan, did you know?

Gerald R. Ford, who grew up in
Grand Rapids, was the 38th president
of the United States of America.
Before that, he was a University of
Michigan football star, served on a
World War II aircraft carrier, and
represented Michigan in Congress
for 24 years.

Michigan is known as "the Great Lakes State." It is bordered by four of the five Great Lakes, which are the greatest supply of fresh water in the world. To help you remember all five of the Great Lakes, think of the word HOMES, which stands for Huron, Ontario, Michigan, Erie, and Superior.

G is for our Great Lakes,
with water fresh and clear.
To see a state that's edged in blue
just take a good look here.

Michigan is full of wonder, and now you can see why...
Let's turn the page and take a peek at the letters H and I!

H is for the Harbors
filled with boats and lights and docks.
Some are soft and sandy,
and some are filled with rocks.

I is for the Islands.
There are many to be found—
a piece of land that's big or small
with water all around.

Boaters use lighthouses to safely navigate
around shallow or rocky areas and into
harbors. Michigan has more lighthouses
and more registered boats than any
other state.

Michigan has hundreds of islands—
Beaver, Drummond, Grand, and
Mackinac, to name a few. The largest is
Isle Royale in Lake Superior, which is the
northernmost point of the state.

The beautiful Isle Royale greenstone is
our state gem.

Produced in Chelsea, "Jiffy" was the world's first prepared baking mix. Mrs. Mable White Holmes came up with the idea to produce a foolproof baking mix so anyone could bake homemade-quality biscuits and muffins quickly.

J

j

J is for the Jiffy Mix, a quick and easy treat.

And the letter K is for Kellogg.
They make breakfast good to eat.
Crunch, Crunch. Mmmmm...

The Kellogg Company has made Battle Creek "the Cereal Capital of the World." The Kellogg brothers accidentally discovered the process for producing flaked cereal products in their search for healthy foods and sparked the beginning of the dry cereal industry.

Lansing starts with the letter L.
It's the capital of our state.
Here the rules and laws are made
that make Michigan so great.

In the 1600s, Sault Ste. Marie was
an important area for trade, and as
the first European settlement, it
was the region's first capital. In
1805, Detroit became the capital of
the Michigan Territory. Michigan
became a state on January 26,
1837, and Detroit remained the
capital for another ten years. Then
in 1847, after much debate,
Lansing was awarded the honor of
being the state capital of Michigan.

The Lower Peninsula of Michigan is shaped like a mitten. Its unique shape, which is almost entirely surrounded by water, is due to the movement of glaciers, which carved gigantic lake basins and then melted to fill them thousands of years ago.

Now we have a special letter. I'm sure you'll understand.

M is for Mitten, the shape of our land. To see Lower Michigan just hold up your hand.

M m

N is for the Native people,
paddling in the North
and for the Northern Lights,
flashing back and forth.

The word Anishinaabe means "the first people of the land." Native people have lived here for thousands of years, and some of their inventions include the toboggan, the snowshoe, and the birch bark canoe. Michigan's Anishinaabe are known as the Three Fires People: the Chippewa (Ojibwa), Ottawa (Odawa), and Potawatomi (Bodowadomi).

N n

Ore boats, some over three football fields long, carry iron ore, copper, gravel, gypsum, coal, salt, and limestone from Michigan's mines to the industrial cities of the Midwestern United States and throughout the world.

And O is for the Ore boats
that cross our lakes with pride.
They carry precious cargo
to and from the ocean wide.

O o

# P p

P will stand for Painted turtle
floating out of reach,
and also for Petoskey stone,
hiding on the beach.

The Petoskey stone is the official state stone of Michigan. It is a fossil from before the age of the dinosaurs, and is only found in Michigan. Petoskey stones look like ordinary stones when they are dry, but when they are wet you can see their grayish honeycomb pattern. Some people like to find these stones and polish them to a smooth, shiny, brownish-gray color.

Did you know the painted turtle is our state reptile?

Q is for the Quadricycle
rumbling near and far.
With just four wheels and one small seat
it was Henry Ford's first car.

Henry Ford's first gas-powered automobile was named the Quadricycle. He built the engine in his kitchen and completed the Quadricycle in a small shed. To get his 1896 invention out of the shed, he had to knock down a wall because it would not fit through the door.

The red-breasted robin is our state bird. Its song goes, "Tyeep tut-tut-tut."

r

R

R is for the Robin,
with red upon her breast,
singing in the springtime
to the babies in her nest.

Sand dunes are beautiful mounds of windblown sand. Living among the dunes are grasses, plants, trees, and the threatened Dwarf Lake Iris, our state wildflower. The western shore of Michigan has many dunes, including the Sleeping Bear Dunes, which rise 460 feet above Lake Michigan.

Now S is for our Sand dunes,
drifting near the shore.
When the wind begins to blow,
they change their shapes once more.

Michigan has over 150 waterfalls, most of which are in the Upper Peninsula. Tahquamenon Falls is the largest and most recognized of these, and has two waterfalls. The Upper Falls drop nearly 50 feet and are more than 200 feet wide, while the Lower Falls have an island in the middle with five separate cascades on each side. The water gets its rich copper color from the decaying vegetation in nearby swamps.

Tahquamenon begins with T,
two waterfalls on a river.
The water rushes by so fast
it almost makes us quiver!

Oooh, what a sight...
falling, falling, with all of its might!

U

Upper Peninsula begins with U,
rugged beauty for all to see.
Lakes and rivers, ponds and streams
are part of the great U.P.

The Upper Peninsula is renowned
for its natural beauty of mountains,
rivers, lakes, forests, and wildlife. It
is also rich in resources, particularly
copper, iron ore, and timber.

Can you see the shape of a running
rabbit when you look at the Upper
Peninsula?

Vernors, created in Detroit, was the first soda pop made in the United States. In 1862, pharmacist James Vernor was trying to make a new drink when he was called to serve our country in the Civil War. He left his secret concoction in an oak cask. When he returned home four years later, he discovered that his drink had acquired a delicious gingery flavor. And the rest is pop history!

Make a cool, refreshing treat by mixing Vernors with ice cream!

**Vernors**

*America's first Soda*

Vernors is a soda pop that starts with the letter V. The first one made in the U.S.A., it's as tasty as can be.

Fizz, Fizz!

W is for White-tailed deer
as well as Wolverine.
Wherever you are in Michigan,
there's wildlife to be seen.

Michigan is nicknamed "the Wolverine State," and is a wonderland full of winter adventures, such as skiing and snowshoeing. The white-tailed deer is the state mammal and is a graceful creature of the forest.

Did you know deer shed their antlers each year?

W
W

The letter X marks the spot
where ships have met their fate.
Deep beneath the water
sunken boats and treasure wait.

Thousands of ships have crashed or sunk in the waters that border Michigan. Two of the most noted are the "Griffin," which sank on its maiden voyage in 1679, and the "Edmund Fitzgerald," a huge ore boat that sank in 1975 and was later immortalized in the song *The Wreck of the Edmund Fitzgerald.*

Xx

The Chicago to Mackinac Yacht Race is the oldest and longest freshwater yacht race in the world. Sailors have been challenging the unpredictable waters of Lake Michigan since the first race in 1898.

Y is for the many Yachts
that race along the lake.
Some are slow and quiet.
Some leave a great big wake!

Z is for the Detroit Zoo.
It's fun as fun can be.
Now you've discovered Michigan
from the letters A to Z.

The Detroit Zoo was the first zoo in America to feature cageless, open exhibits that allow the animals more freedom to roam. The famous "Bear Hill" was the first exhibit of this type and today it remains a favorite among children of all ages.

# A Mitten Full of Facts

1. Do you know Michigan's state motto?

2. The Upper Peninsula of Michigan has the only true mountain range located between the Allegheny Mountains and the Rocky Mountains. Do you know the name of this mountain range?

3. This is the only community in Michigan over which the flags of four countries have flown. This community is located in the southwestern region of Michigan. Can you name the community? Can you name the four countries?

4. Which president of the United States was the first to call the people in Michigan "Michiganders"?

5. In 1870, Detroit was the first city in the nation to get what? Hint: Almost everyone has one, some have more than one.

6. What is the name of the longest river in Michigan?

7. Michigan makes the most of this condiment in the nation. What is it?

8. You have read about Michigan's state bird and state flower. Michigan also has a state soil. Do you know what it is called? Hint: There is a town located just east of Traverse City with the same name.

9. Which of the five Great Lakes is the deepest?

10. Michigan's state seal is on the state flag. There are three animals on the state seal. Can you name these three animals?

11. Which of the five Great Lakes is the shallowest?

12. The world's first car tunnel connecting two countries is in our state. Do you know which two cities and which two countries it connects?

13. Do you know what the man raising his hand on the state seal means?

14. What were the first cars often called?

15. There is an area of the Saint Mary's River that connects Lake Superior and Lake Huron. Boats needed a way to bypass the rapids on the river. What was built in 1855 to make the bypass possible?

16. Michigan became the 26th state of the Union in 1837. Do you know how many stars were sewn on the American Flag at that time?

**17.** Michigan has been called a "Water Wonderland." Do you know how many inland lakes there are in Michigan?

**18.** Wherever you are in Michigan you are within how many miles of a body of water?

**19.** Michigan's first governor, Stevens T. Mason, was 24 years old when he took office. What was his nickname?

**20.** Why is Michigan nicknamed the "Wolverine State?" Hint: There are two explanations.

## Annie Appleford

Annie Appleford is a lifelong resident of Michigan. Annie's love for Michigan inspired her to create a Michigan alphabet book. Born and raised in a suburb of Detroit, she spent the summers of her youth at a family cottage on the shore of Lake Michigan. A dedicated and ardent Michigander, Annie received her undergraduate degree from the University of Michigan and a Master of Elementary Education from Eastern Michigan University. She lives in northern lower Michigan with her husband, daughter, and son.

## Kathy-jo Wargin

Author Kathy-jo Wargin believes that young children learn best when they are having fun—and what could be more fun than learning the Michigan ABC's in a series of playful rhymes and facts? She is also the author of *The Legend of Mackinac Island* and *The Legend of Sleeping Bear*. Kathy-jo lives with her husband Ed and her son Jake in Harbor Springs, Michigan, where she can proudly say **H** is for the Harbors, filled with boats and lights and docks, some are soft and sandy, and some are filled with rocks.

## Michael G. Monroe

Self-taught artist Michael Monroe spends most of his time exploring the outdoors and honing his first love, his wildlife artwork. Michael enjoys experimenting with a variety of unique painting techniques to bring to life the magic of natural moments. He has received extensive recognition for his wildlife paintings, including the Michigan Wildlife Artist of the Year award and the Michigan Duck Stamp award. His work on *M is for Mitten: A Michigan Alphabet* has focused his talents toward a new audience, children. He cites as his inspiration for this challenge his two children, Natalie and Matthew.